THE WOODLAND HOUSE

Ben Law

Published by

Permanent Publications
Hyden House Ltd
The Sustainability Centre
East Meon
Hampshire GU32 1HR
England
Tel: 01730 823 311
Fax: 01730 823 322
Overseas: (international code +44 - 1730)
Email: enquiries@permaculture.co.uk
Web: www.permaculture.co.uk

Designed and typeset by John Adams

Front cover photograph by Steve Morley

Back cover photograph by Ben Law

Printed by CPI Bath

Printed on Totally Chlorine Free paper

British Library Cataloguing-in-Publication Data

A catalogue record for this book is available from the British Library

ISBN 1 85623 031 7

THE
WOODLAND
HOUSE

CONTENTS

Until One Is Committed

Until one is committed, there is hesitancy, the chance to
draw back, always in effectiveness. Concerning all acts
of initiative (and creation) there is one elementary truth,
the ignorance of which kills countless ideas and splendid
plans: that the moment one definitely commits oneself,
then providence moves too. All sorts of things occur to
help one that would otherwise never have occurred.
A whole stream of events issues from the decision,
raising in one's favour all manner of unforeseen
incidents and meetings and material assistance,
which no man could have dreamed would
have come his way.

Whatever you can do, or dream you can, begin it.
Boldness has genius, power and magic in it.

Johann Wolfgang Von Goethe

Foreword

KEVIN McCLOUD

Ben Law is an extraordinary man. Not exactly a warrior for his cause, more the quiet victor. Ben has proved that it's possible to make a good living as an underwoodsman – coppicing, hurdle making and charcoal burning, simply by working hard and applying good commercial business sense. He's also proved that it's possible to design and construct an elegant, sophisticated and truly environmentally-friendly home from materials around you, providing you design with diligence and sensitivity. And he has proved beyond a shadow of a doubt that great architecture need not be urban, or glamorous or loud.

I first met Ben when filming the third series of *Grand Designs* for Channel 4. We followed over a year the steady, measured construction of his house and watched coppiced chestnut being willed into a new form as a dwelling. It was clear then that because of Ben's highly unusual planning circumstances and the exceptional nature of his job and skills that came with it, we were witnessing something rare; an event in building that doesn't happen at all often. And in the three years since, we have not been able to find a project with the equivalent integrity of man, material and design. I suspect we won't for a long time.

Sustainable is a word that in the last few years has become almost meaningless. It's now so overworn a word, it's become so floppy you can take it and stuff it with whatever you like: organic straw; urethane foam insulation or just hot air. Whenever I need to remind myself what the word

really means, I think of Ben's house and how we managed to make a film about sustainable construction whilst mentioning the word just once. Here is a house so ecologically sound, it breathes in time to the trees around it. Nearly every bit of wood in the place (and it is nigh all wood) grew in that forest and was coppiced. The subsequent coppice stumps or stools are now regrowing so fast and gulping in their youth so much carbon dioxide, that within a few years the environmental impact of constructing and living in this building will have been more than outweighed. Putting it into hard environmental

language, this, in carbon terms, is an invisible house.

But it mustn't remain too invisible because it's also a beautiful house and one that answers eloquently to its setting. Ben has a shrewd eye for design, proportion and the subtleties of colour and materials. The result is a delightful building which appears as rooted as it can possibly be; one, that like all good architecture, responds intelligently to both its context and to human beings. Ben's home has been made out of its very context, by him. You couldn't find a house that has a more intimate relationship with people and place.

WHY BUILD?

Chapter One

Finishing walking sticks in the outdoor kitchen, with many aspects of woodland life on show.

I grew up building camps in the wood. Unknown to me as a child I was experimenting with my instinct to build. I built camps out of twigs and grass, some were just places I could fit into, but to me they were camps. Some were in trees, one was in the top of an ancient yew hedge. I would spend hours there watching people coming and going, the best part was the exit which involved sliding down the outside of the hedge. One winter we had snowdrifts, the wind had blown the snow against the hedges and we made caves in the snowdrifts. I remember making my first straw house, I must have been about seven at the time. The footpath at the top of the lane was an old track and it bisected a large arable field. The straw was bailed and stacked in piles of about sixteen bales, far too tempting for a boy on a summer evening. I restacked the bales leaving a small entrance to crawl through into my little bale house. Thirty years later I have built my second straw bale house.

Building camps and making structures has never left me. Shelter is a basic need, the survival instinct that should be available to everyone. Society has put a price upon it and made many people unable to afford this essential human need. For most of us this is the biggest expense of our lives, whether owned or rented.

Twelve years ago I moved into the woods and built myself a bender, a structure made of bent hazel poles covered in tarpaulins. I paid fifty pounds for a heavy-duty hemp tarpaulin and it was a home I could afford. I moved into the woods because of instinct, the need to live closer to nature and become more connected and in tune with the rhythms of the countryside. Woodlands have always made me feel at home. The trees themselves create forms of shelter, many a time I have crawled across the spiky leaves of a holly tree to find a dry place to shelter in a torrential rainstorm.

My first woodland bender was simple enough and about eight feet wide and fifteen feet long. It had a wood burning stove, a bed, table, some cushions and a large window looking across the clearing. I have fond memories of my first woodland home.

Living within the woodland I was able to observe and build up a picture of other creatures living there, while I cut the coppice and worked through the night burning wood to make charcoal.

One day I returned to my canvas dwelling to find an envelope stapled to the canvas. It was from my local planning authority. Apparently I was in breach of planning law. "How can this be?" I thought. Charcoal burners have always lived in structures they have built themselves in the woods. And so began an exhausting number of years as I entered into the process of learning about planning law, how it works and where I stood as a forest dweller under law.

My response was to keep moving

my dwelling around and vary the type of dwelling I was living in. Meanwhile correspondence and planning deadlines came and went. I built and lived in a second bender, then a small caravan, then a Mongolian yurt, and then I bought in a mobile home. It was no easy task moving a thirty-foot static caravan with small wheels across uneven ground to its new position. The static caravan seemed totally out of place in a woodland setting but with the help of a rustic veranda it didn't look too bad during the summer months when the leaves of the chestnut broke up the boxy-ness of its shape. I applied for a temporary planning permission and the caravan (commonly used for temporary permissions in agricultural situations) fitted into the right box and my temporary permission was granted.

Three years later after further building up my woodland business (coppice management and adding value through craftwork and construction) and expanding the area under my stewardship, I applied for a full planning permission.

After much discussion at the development control committee meeting of the local planning authority the application was approved. It was not until I received the written approval, that I noticed one particular clause, which seemed at best to be exceedingly unfair.

This clause in allowing me permission to build a house also stated that if I lost control of any of the land I managed – and this involved land owned by two adjacent neighbours – I would have to pull down my house. What this really meant was if one of my neighbours moved house and somebody else bought that house who did not want me to continue managing their woods, I would have to pull down my house. This seemed rather draconian to me. I could not think of any other example whereby if one's neighbour moved and somebody else moved in who perhaps did not want you to work on their land you had to have your house pulled down. I therefore challenged this draconian planning clause and was very grateful that I was successful and the clause was quashed from the planning application. I felt more comfortable being able to build a house knowing that if one of neighbours moved I would be able to keep the house.

Top Left:
The bender that was Ben's first home on the site.

Bottom Left:
Charcoal burners' huts near Haslemere, Surrey.

Above:
English woodland version of a Mongolian yurt. Blends in well and is not very different from a traditional charcoal burners dwelling.

THE DESIGN PROCESS
Orientation
Available Materials
Services
Skills
Drawings

Chapter Two

Small veranda outside the kitchen door.

I have been fortunate enough to study and put into practice design through the principles of permaculture for a number of years. The drawn out planning struggles I encountered have had one benefit, that of giving me many years to observe the land and consider the type of house that would be suitable for my lifestyle. Most houses are designed by architects who discuss the needs of their clients with them, make a site visit or two and come up with a plan. My house was designed by me after ten years of observing and getting to know the site I was going to build on. I knew the soil types, aspects, seasonal wind directions, my patterns of work within the wood, and the requirements which the house I was going to live in would need to serve. Added to this I knew the type of materials available to me to build a house, my own level of skill and a network of friends and contacts. The attempt to design and undertake a self build project felt more likely to succeed under my own guidance than managed by someone with no understanding of my lifestyle or the land itself.

So what does my lifestyle involve? It involves being outside most of the day and therefore the design needed to incorporate a lot of indoor/outdoor spaces – verandas and decks where I can sit at the end of a long day of coppicing before taking off my boots and going inside the house. My work involves working in a variety of conditions. In the winter, the house has to deal with wet weather and muddy tracks and this had a large influence on my designing of the house on stilts so it was clear of the ground all the way around it. In summer, the woods become hot and dusty and

places to sit in the shade become much more of a priority. Autumn and spring are the windows of balance between the wet and muddy and the dry and dusty periods, when the woodland is at its most beautiful and also climatically balanced to live within.

My winter work involves cutting coppice, hedge laying, cleaving chestnut poles, pruning fruit trees and, by the end of the day, whatever I am wearing usually has a good coating of sawdust, leaf litter and mud. There would be no point in me stepping inside onto a thick pile carpet. What suits my lifestyle is a floor I can sweep, so sawdust is allowed to freely fall and can be swept up with a few brushes of a broom.

I have lived for a number of years with an attempted 'shoes off' policy. Since spending time travelling in Asia, I realised how strange it is to walk off the street into someone's house with just a faint scuff on a door mat, and to carry on in that same pair of shoes wandering around someone's home. There is a certain respect when you remove your shoes at someone's door. After all, you are being invited into the heart of their personal space. So I will

try to encourage a 'no shoes' ideal in the house I design and common sense amplifies this when you see the thick layer of mud around my boots at the end of a day's work in winter. To make your shoes-off house work well in an English climate, there needs to be a comfortable covered indoor/outdoor space to remove your shoes in the dry, so that the change is both comfortable and also encourages people to adhere to it.

As the winter begins to fade and

Top Left:
The mobile home on the site of the new house.

Bottom Left:
Covered outdoor kitchen area.

Above:
The home clearing looking North.

the soil starts to dry out, places to sit and contemplate my summer plans for the woods become more important. Shoes and boots become less relevant, only being worn for outdoor work and occasional jaunts into town. Visitors become more frequent and the need for sitting areas in the sun and the shade becomes apparent. Large spaces for eating or socialising and smaller niches for intimate one-to-one conversations or for that quiet moment alone are important. All these aspects of my lifestyle can be incorporated into well designed indoor/outdoor spaces. These transition spaces where one passes from the outside to the inside as if passing through changing worlds, a kind of dawn or dusk between day and night, the beach between land and sea, these are likely to be the most used spaces in the whole house design.

Orientation

I have lived in both a yurt and a caravan on the site where I am going to build the house, so I not only have ten years of site orientation study but also the experience of understanding the patterns of light movement throughout the year on the exact spot where I will be living. I have chosen east-west orientation with gable ends to the north and the south. Not ideal for storing large solar panels on the southern side, but chosen because of the lay of the land and the positioning of the building in relation to other structures in the clearing, my work shop and summer kitchen. The slope I am building on drops four and a half feet to the east over a twenty foot span. This allows me to design on stilts and have all the plumbing running along the eastern side of the house. This will be easy to access and

can be comfortably worked on from underneath. The slope continues allowing gravity to carry grey water through a reed bed purification system.

The composting toilet is situated on the north-eastern corner, the coolest part of the house, and again there is plenty of room beneath the house to empty the toilet from outside.

The kitchen is in the south-eastern corner of the house, with a large eastern window and window seat to catch the first rays of sunlight, even on the coldest days. The back door opens from the kitchen onto a covered deck, the perfect spot for a sunny breakfast.

The main living room is large and open plan and receives light through windows from the east, south and west as well as six roof lights. This ensures that the house is filled with light at all times of the year. Having lived in many green canvas structures, I have spent too many years in poor light, so filling the house with light is a key part of the design.

The main doors open out to the west

onto a covered veranda. This is the perfect place to catch the last of the sun (which leaves me early since the site is on the north-east face of the hill) and relax at the end of a working day. This veranda continues along the south of the building and links up with the breakfast deck outside the back door. I may construct a pergola over the southern deck and grow grapes and kiwi fruit, giving me a dappled shade in the summer and allowing the low winter sun to pour into the house unhindered, falling onto the clay walls as part of the passive solar heating.

As I mentioned before, the sun leaves me earlier than I would like it to, and so an upstairs balcony on the southern gable, open to the east and west sun, ensures I can extend time in the sun once it has left the western veranda. Thinking about light, the winter and summer extremes of sun, and where you would like to be at different times of the day, are key parts to getting the building orientated successfully in the landscape, and ensuring it meets your living needs.

Available Materials

I live in the middle of a woodland. The woodland is predominantly sweet chestnut coppice. Sweet chestnut is a very durable, fast growing hardwood. I built a small cruck frame boathouse with Viv Goodings and Mark Jones a few years previously and it was the joy of using roundwood sweet chestnut for timber framing that gave me the desire to build a house from the most sustainable timber resource available – coppice wood. Having the timber available to build the house not only reduced the cost of buying in materials, but also removed transport costs and the common problem of not having the materials on site that you need. It also saved greatly on the environmental impact of the house, not having to transport the majority of the materials to the building site. The other material I have available in the wood is clay. The pond at the bottom of the woods used to be a catchment pond for Lodsworth Brickworks. I knew from when I renovated the pond nine years earlier that there was a good seam of quality clay available so I had the material I needed for the inside walls and the fireplace. I needed York stone slabs for the foundations and after asking around my local pubs, I had been given enough stone for all forty-two pad stones, plus a few extra for around the fireplace. The ancient farm at Butser offered me five tonnes of surplus lime putty and sand and so this led to the inevitable use of straw bales. After asking local farmers and friends, I eventually tracked down Paul Mills from nearby Chiddingfold, who still makes small size straw bales. So my main materials for the build were either available from the woodland itself or from local sources.

Services

I had been living without mains electricity for ten years, and the caravan had a basic twelve volt system running from a couple of solar panels and wind turbines. To bring mains electricity to the woods would be impractical from the point of distance, and also because cables below ground would disturb tree roots and any over ground cables would make the felling of coppice more awkward. I am also used to living with limited amounts of twelve volt electricity, so it is easier for me to expand my solar bank and continue with a twelve volt system.

I have collected rainwater off the caravan roof and I have always been amazed at the volume of water one can collect. If you take the surface area of the roof and multiply it by the average annual rainfall you will get an estimate of the volume of water you can expect per annum. The important part of a successful rain water system is enough surface area of roof and enough storage capacity for the water. I have bartered a thousand gallon water tank in return for laying a hedge and this is more than sufficient for my needs throughout the year. The rainwater will be used for hot and cold running water for washing up, baths, showers and watering the garden but not for drinking. Drinking water comes from a spring and well.

Wastewater from the sink and bath is known as grey water. With the pull of gravity, it will move through a series of reed beds that will purify the water on its journey towards the pond. My toilet will be a compost loo with interchangeable tanks beneath the house. I have lived with a composting loo and been very pleased with the quality of compost it makes, which in turn gets spread around my fruit trees and helps ensure bumper crops of fruit. The house is designed to be self sufficient in dealing

Left:
Cruck framed boathouse.

Above:
The clay pond in the woods.

with services coming in and out. By generating electricity from the wind and sun, summer hot water from the sun, winter hot water from wood from the coppice, purifying grey water and turning the contents of my toilet into manure, those brown envelopes that come through the door have become few and far between. I will also be living in the knowledge that the impact on the environment from my house is minimal.

Skills

The most important skill I had to build the house was the belief that I could do it. Once you believe that you can do something, you are well on the way to doing it! I have a good selection of practical skills and know the timber well that I am using in the build. I can fell trees, peel them, cleave them and joint them together, therefore I have the basics of being able to build a timber framed house. I have experience of organising projects and know the importance of good preparation and site management to make a project succeed. I am not afraid to ask for help if I need it and have built up a large network of people who I can call upon to help. So with that as a background, I was confident that either I had the skills myself, or I could find someone with the skills to ensure this project would succeed.

Drawings

My design for the house came from the cruck frame, one of the earliest timber frame designs. This is a series of 'A' frames which are raised and linked together with a ridgepole and wall plates. I built a cruck frame boathouse and at that time knew I wanted to build a dwelling using these beautiful curved pieces of wood. I did some rough sketches and then sat down one evening with Susana

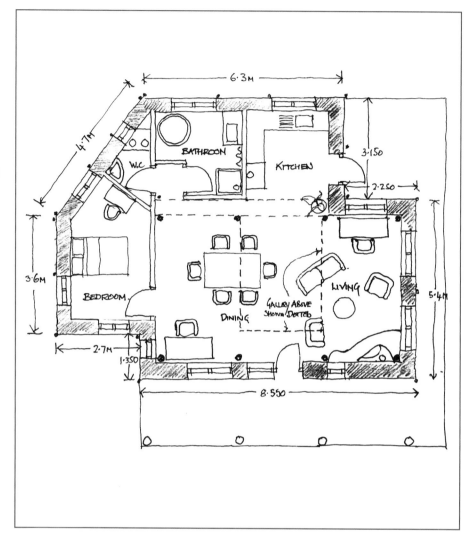

Laughton, an architect student, and she turned them into initial scale drawings. Afterwards, I consulted Constructive Individuals, a specialist team of ecological architects, who took my drawings and created a full set of aspects and cross sections suitable for application to the local planning authority. I also made a very rustic model which helped me to see in three dimensions how the building would fit together, and later John Rees from Constructive Individuals constructed a detailed scale model which proved invaluable during the the early stages of the build.

Above:
Layout plan.

Top Right:
Front elevation (West).

Bottom Right:
Rear elevation (East).

Further drawings including elevations, sections, foundation and bale plans can be found in Appendix VI, page 85.

BUILDING
REGULATIONS

Chapter Three

The house shortly after completion of the main structure with Ben's dog Oilly in the foreground.

With planning approved I was ready to start building, but there was one more major hurdle to overcome before beginning – getting approval of the engineering of my design by building control. Building regulations that fall under Building Regulation 1991, Section Sixteen, of the Building Act 1984, are in place to ensure that a building is constructed to a safe and satisfactory standard. In more recent years legislation has been tightened up on the energy efficiency of new homes, thereby ensuring new homes are well insulated, double glazed and more energy efficient. This is a positive part of the regulations and a step forward from an environmental perspective. Where the regulations (similar to all legal requirements I have come across) fall down, in my opinion, is the lack of flexibility for different circumstances and types of buildings. For example, there is no variation in allowances for urban and rural situations, although house type, access, etc is often very different. There

is also no flexibility for the self-builder, who is unlikely to build a house that will fall down as he or she has got to live in it.

With my house, I knew the sizes of timber I wanted to use for each part of the building, and I cut them according to my visual understanding and experience of sweet chestnut. Five hundred years ago, people would have gone into the forest, cut timber and built a house, no-one would have questioned the stresses and loads upon the timber. Many of those timber framed buildings of five hundred years ago and before are still standing, a testament to people who understood wood and got on and built with it.

I understand wood, and with mine cut and ready to go, I was drawn into a process that lasted four months. This involved meetings, phone calls and letters, and cost me a lot of money. I had to employ John Rees from Constructive Individuals to come and help me sort out building regulations, as I had no experience of them and I

found the list of compliances and the use of jargon in the regulations difficult for the lay person to understand. John compiled outline specifications and after we had agreed them, he submitted the regulation notes.

I, meanwhile, designed the composting toilet system and the reed bed system and obtained approval from the environment agency. Then I had to meet up with a fire officer, to ensure it was possible to service the building and gained approval to pass fire regulations. Meanwhile, John Dash of Jeffrey Smith Associates, construction engineers who John Rees was acquainted with, slowly worked on the calculations for using sweet chestnut in the round. The only way of calculating the bending, tension, compression, sheering and elasticity of the roundwood, was to either set up physical tests (a very expensive process) or to use the data available from British Research Establishment *Digest 445*. In this paper, it shows figures for sweet chestnut to be very similar

to that of oak but, the figures were for sawn wood. There were no figures for roundwood. John worked on the maximum size of square section he could take from the roundwood pole and then ran the calculations. One or two of my poles failed slightly in deflection, but this was for sawn wood.

As a woodsman, I know very well that the moment a roundwood pole is sawn it loses considerable strength, as the fibres have been severed. After talking with a member of the department of wood science at Surrey University, who had experimented testing roundwood poles, he confirmed that timber in the round is approximately fifty percent stronger

in bending and deflection than the equivalent sawn square section. So the poles I had cut comfortably passed the testing and building control was content that the structure had been tested by an engineer.

This process held up the build for four months and cost me approximately £1,500 in fees to the architect and the engineer so they could prove to building control that the poles I had already cut and knew would be fine for the build were indeed fine. The information worked out by the engineer is available in *Appendix VII,* so that if you would like to build with sweet chestnut in the round, you can use these figures and save the cost of hiring an engineer.

Above:
The model of the house allowed the project to be viewed in three dimensions.

Left:
Some of the chestnut poles needed for the roundwood framing.

PREPARATION

Site Access

Materials Needed

The Roundwood Timber Frame

Straw Bales

Doors

Window Frames

Pegs

Shingles

Clay

Lime

Fixings

Bale Spikes

Mobile Sawmills

Tools

Volunteers

Health & Safety

Budget

Chapter Four

Peeling the bark from a pole. Every piece of roundwood had to be shaved in this way.

Site Access

The access to my woodland is not straightforward. I have forestry access across my neighbour's field and then there is a rough sandstone track through the woodland before arriving at the building plot. The field has a heavy clay soil and can become difficult to traverse even with a four-wheel drive, after heavy rain. So I was well aware of the importance of getting all materials to the plot while the weather was fine or the ground was hard from frost in the winter.

Fortunately most of my materials were coming directly from the woodland itself, however there were some others like large dumpy sacks of lime that had to be brought across the field. Working on the land soon teaches you the ancient art of 'timeliness' – getting the hay in before it rains, extracting the timber before the frost breaks up. Using the few windows of the right weather to get work completed on the land was good preparation for ensuring poor access would not hold up the build.

Materials Needed

To work out the materials I needed and also to help prepare a budget, I got a large sheet of flip chart paper and I brainstormed, first randomly writing down the key things that I knew I needed for the build and then expanding on them in more detail. For example, timber cladding for the walls evolved into oak or chestnut cladding and that in turn made me consider how I would fix it. In this case it was to be stainless steel fixings onto a large stud frame, and then the whole process for the walls began to take shape. Straw bales, lime plaster, breathable membrane… against all these components I made a note of whether I already had them or where I could get them and an idea of cost. I then worked with the scaled drawings of the plans to begin to quantify volumes. So through the

brainstorming process, I mapped the materials I needed and went mentally through the building process. It was a useful and important process but it is not the same as the reality of building and there were a few materials I overlooked.

The Roundwood Timber Frame

I located the main crucks for the timber frame in a nearby wood and they were transported by tractor and trailer to the site. The rest of the frame came out of Prickly Nut Wood itself (my home and working woodland) and I had already marked particular trees for a specific purpose. The ridgepole was over thirty two feet long and needed to be very straight. When examining standing trees it is easy to be deceived by what looks straight as a vertical pole, only to find it kinks or curves once it is laid out on the ground in a horizontal position. I cut more than I needed and marked the key poles for the frame, so that they didn't get used elsewhere during the build. Once they were all stacked at the build site, it seemed amazing to think that this pile of over two hundred coppice poles would end up becoming a house.

Straw Bales

Having decided to construct the walls from straw, I set about trying to locate a good source, so that I had baled straw stored and ready prior to the beginning the build. I tried my most local farmers, but to my dismay I found that none of them still used a small size baler and they all made large bales, moveable only by machine not people. Through my network of friends and colleagues, I was put onto Paul Mills who farmed nearby and still made small size bales. He had already stored, in a barn, a good quantity of barley straw bales. I ordered three hundred and fifty and Paul agreed to keep them in the barn until nearer the time that I needed them. By keeping them in the barn they were naturally compacting and therefore would not subside when used in the building.

My use of bales was as infill between the main roundwood frame and the stud wall which would be weather boarded. The bales therefore had no load bearing responsibility in the building and so I was content to use barley straw bales. Had the building had any load bearing on the straw bales I would have searched for wheat straw, as it is more stable in a load bearing building. Straw bale building is still a fairly new concept in the UK. In Australia and America, however, it is a well-documented technique. The big difference I see in using bales in the UK is the large amount of rainfall we can have, and that to protect the bales in as many ways as possible is the best solution.

The use of lime plaster, which is weather proof, seals the bales from fire and also works as a rodenticide, keeping away mice. Another part of the solution is a web of boarded stud wall with an air gap, and another is to have overhangs sheltering the bale walls, like the covered veranda I have on the west aspect of the house. I used a combination of all these techniques to maintain a bale wall which keeps moisture from coming into the bale but is breathable to let any moisture escape.

Doors

There are not many doors in my design as it is very open plan. There are three internal doors and two external ones. My original plan was to make most of the doors myself but while hedgelaying in the winter prior to starting my build, I noticed that one of the nearby houses was having major building works. One large external oak door was in a skip and hand made oak internal doors were leaning against the house. I obtained these doors for a small consideration. The front door of the house I already had, having acquired it by barter seven years previously. It was a large oak barn door and my plan was to cut it down the middle, add extra bracing and have a set of double opening doors.

Window Frames

I searched through many ecological building brochures in the hope of finding some local English hardwood windows at a sensible price. They do not exist as far as I know so I went and visited my friend Tim Boxley, cabinetmaker and furniture

Left:
Using a draw knife and shaving horse to prepare timber for turning into framing pegs.

Above:
Side axing a piece of ash. Once squared up it was machined into a window frame component.

either direction. The oak was sawn to about one and a quarter inch by one and a quarter inch. Then I worked on a shaving horse with a drawknife to turn the wood cylindrical. Then I used a rounding plane, which is like a giant pencil sharpener to create dowels of one inch, three quarters of an inch and five eighths of an inch depending on the strength of the joint needed. Working with roundwood for timber framing rather than traditional squared green oak meant we used mainly cylindrical pegs with wedges for the type of joints we created rather than 'draw pegs'.

Shingles or Shakes

I did my first shingled roof on a boathouse three years prior to the build and I totally fell for the beautiful almost reptilian scales which appeared

restorer, and asked him what he knew about making windows. He had never made them before but was up for the challenge.

The only available timber I had was chestnut or ash. Chestnut would be more durable but was more likely to move and split and all the wood was a fair way from being seasoned. So we opted for ash and I turned up at Tim's workshop with a pick up full of lengths of ash in the round. "But these are logs," exclaimed Tim. "Yes," I replied with a smile, "They are all I have." So I used wedges to cleave the logs apart and then a side axe to try and get something close to a flat face on the wood before we put them onto the planer and started to machine them into suitable dimensions.

The size of the windows had been designed around the dimensions of the bale walls so a large window was one bale wide by three bales high. The machining seemed to take days and I was glad we had begun the process six

months before the build began. We ended up with kit windows of sawn planed ash, and left them to season more before jointing them together. As Tim and I jointed the first small window together, I can clearly remember the feeling of total satisfaction. We had started with coppiced ash I had felled in the winter and now we had a beautiful ash window frame. For Tim, there were another thirteen windows to join together as by that time I was managing the build. Being ash, the windows needed to be treated against the weather and for this we used Timberdura, a mixture of beeswax and linseed oil.

Pegs

To fix the main frame together, we used wooden pegs or dowels. For these I chose seasoned oak, so that the green chestnut frame would shrink tightly around the peg and make a firm joint. The pegs were then wedged both sides to ensure that they could not move in on the roof. I knew I wanted to shingle my house when I built it and estimated I would need about ten thousand. These I obtained from a local woodsman but I was still two thousand short which I split out myself with a froe. I would have liked to have made them all but this would have delayed the build by another fifty days as two hundred a day is my present limit! The shingles that I made are what are known as 'bastard' shingles. These have not been split radially from a log, they have been made by squaring off a bit of roundwood and splitting slices off it with a froe, discarding the very central core of the log as this will split. They were then finished by tapering them with a drawknife and putting a bevel on the opened weathered end of the shingle. Chestnut is wonderful for making bastard shingles as it has so little sapwood. This means shingles can easily be made from quite small diameter roundwood, six inches and above.

"Surplus wood fed the fire that boiled the kettle and cooked the food that fed the workers that built the house that Ben built."

Top Left:
Tim Boxley machining a window frame in his workshop.

Bottom Left:
Trying out the roofing shingles.

Top:
Making pegs with a rounding plane, which work like a pencil sharpener.

Centre:
A pegged joint showing the wedges which jam the pegs in place.

Bottom:
Ben pegging a main frame joint.

Clay

When I arrived at Prickly Nut Wood there was the silted up remains of what had obviously been a pond on the woodland edge. I cleared the rubbish, re-using what I could, hired a digger and dumper and re-dug the pond. As I dug I was impressed by the quality of clay available and I experimented making clay ovens, which I still use today. The pond had previously been a catchment pond for the local brickworks, so I was not surprised to find good quality clay. Ten years later I remembered the position of a good seam and Stuart Cameron from the village appeared with his digger on a very wet summers day and we dug out and dumped enough good clay at the site for the internal walls and the fireplace.

Lime

I wanted to use lime on the straw bales because it creates a breathable waterproof layer and also is a partial rodenticide. In other words mice don't like going though it. I have a friend and woodsman, Jonathan West, who is the education officer at Butser open-air museum and he mentioned they had surplus lime putty and sand that they needed to get rid of.

I arranged for a truck to pick it up and five tonnes arrived on site, enough to do over half the house. I knew nothing about working with lime so I went on an excellent one-day course with Mike Wye in Devon, where I learnt how to plaster and understand the importance of the different layers and climatic conditions for drying lime. I also purchased the remaining lime plaster I needed from Mike.

Fixings

The main frame is fixed together with wooden pegs. Other fixings had to be either stainless steel or copper as chestnut, like oak, has the ability to dissolve other fixings over time. The shingles were all pre-drilled and fixed with copper clout nails while the larch floor and roof joists were fixed to the chestnut with five inch stainless steel annular ring shanks. These proved to be the most flexible nails I have ever come across and there was much entertainment during the build seeing how many were bent in the process of trying to secure the joists and rafters. All the fixings were ordered and ready prior to the build as finding unusual nails like five inch stainless steel annular ring shanks can take time, so it is best to be prepared well in advance.

Bale Spikes

The bale spikes were coppiced from four-year-old sweet chestnut the winter prior to the build. They were then hammered through the bales to lock them together. The bottom bale sat

on a metal spike with a plate that was coach screwed into the floor joists giving a solid fixing to the walls. These I had made up by Tony Tonger, who runs a small engineering and fabrication workshop locally.

Mobile Sawmills

I used two mobile mills prior to the build. The first was a Lumber Mate that belongs to Ian Plumer, a local woodsman and we milled up some oak standards I had thinned in the coppice a couple of years previously. These were for the waney edge boards for the outside of the house. There is a small larch plantation in the adjacent woodland I manage where I have begun a fatting operation. Most soft wood plantations are thinned and then the larger trees grown on to an optimum size before a final clear fell. The thinnings are of little value. My operation involves taking out the larger trees and I call it fatting. This allows more light into the woodland so that the thinner trees can grow on. It also encourages natural regeneration of other species. There are a good number of straight ash, oak and birch now well established amongst the plantation. I felled fifteen large trees and Paul D'Barrow arrived with his Wood-Mizer, a mobile sawmill. We milled up all the wood into floor joists in two long wet days.

Tools

I was fortunate to already have many tools that I needed for the build. I purchased a set of large timber framing chisels, a corner chisel, extra drills and hammers, and begged and borrowed most of the other tools I needed. Think carefully about what tools you'll need and try and make sure that you will have everything available before you begin. The build can be held up considerably if a particular tool is not available at a certain time.

Top Left:
The pond proved a valuable source of high quality clay.

Bottom Left:
A Wood-Mizer mobile sawmill, milling

larch for the floor and roof joists.

Above:
Ben cutting chestnut coppice with a lightweight chainsaw. This saw was also used to trim and shape bale walls.

Volunteers

I had no idea how many volunteers would turn up for the build, what skills they would have and how they would adapt to camping in a woodland. I had worked with volunteers before and I had found that to give them responsibility, tell them to have a go at something they hadn't tried before and let them know that if they make a mistake it is OK, went a long way to ensuring everybody had a good experience. (Obviously I was careful not to let them make their first ever mortice into the main frame of the building!).

Volunteers come to learn, to have fun, meet people and experience something new. I never set times for people to start work. I was often building for two hours before volunteers appeared for breakfast, but it is important to appreciate that volunteers are giving their time and labour for the experience. Consequently, I found that many of my volunteers became totally committed to the project, returning again and again, and some even stayed for a few months.

The other really important part of

making a project fun for volunteers is food. Good meals mean happy volunteers. I ended up having almost a hundred volunteers to help in different ways during the build, and the building could not have happened without them. Catering in the woods took place in the

summer kitchen, meals were cooked over an open fire and the evenings were often spent around the fire or down at the local pub!

Health and Safety

It is very easy to become complacent on a building site tucked away in the middle of a wood, with little machinery and usually only a few people actually working on the house at any one time. We therefore set our guidelines. Hard hats were available at all times for everyone. If anyone was working on the roof or above ground level on the building then hard hats were compulsory for anyone below. I had the responsibility of quite often telling people they needed a hard hat and after a while people became more aware. Harnesses were used for roof work and the building work passed without any on site injuries.

A first aid box was always available with a grid reference position of the build taped to the inside of the lid in case of an emergency, and we were fortunate enough to have Vanessa, a qualified nurse, working on the project for a large part of the build.

Budget

I had some previous experience of budgeting projects, but building was a new area for me and therefore rather challenging. I costed up the build to be about twenty five thousand pounds. I allowed a margin for contingencies. I went back to my brainstorming chart and went through the build stage by stage, imagining all I might need and putting a price to it.

I wasn't far out as the build cost, up to the time I started living in the house, was twenty eight thousand pounds. One of the areas I omitted to budget for was the cost of professional services for sorting out building regulations and construction engineering. I put in a nominal figure but had no idea how drawn out the process would be.

Due to the nature of my unusual planning permission I found no mortgage company, including those specialising in ecological self-builds, would lend me the twenty five thousand I needed to cover costs. The fact that the planning stated that the house is for my lifetime only made it an unsafe loan. Eventually Triodos, the ethical Dutch bank based in Bristol, arranged a loan using the land and supportive families as guarantors and loaned me the funds.

It seems most builds are underestimated, so allow large contingencies however thorough and realistic you feel you have been with budgeting. When I look back at the hours and planning I put into preparation before the build, I am confident this played a large part in why the building was finished on time. Many building projects are held up by materials not being available, the craftsmen starting another job, and the whole process consequently becoming delayed. The majority of my materials were sourced and on site prior to the build and others were growing in the woods.

Take time to prepare before beginning. Building the house should be the easy part. It is the managing of the process that will ensure success or failure.

Top Left:
The raising team take a tea break in the outdoor kitchen.

Bottom Left:
Grand Designs *presenter Kevin*

McCloud helps Ben prepare a meal for the volunteers.

Above:
Volunteers having lunch during the shingling stage of construction.

BUILDING AT LAST

Foundations

Preparing The Cruck Frame

The Raise

The Roof

Lean-To Frames

The Floor

Insulation

Straw

Windows

Weatherboarding

Chapter
Five

*Contemplating fixing
the first floorboard.*

Foundations

April was unusually dry and I began by pegging out the site, using a large three by four by five triangle and a string line. Having re-checked all the measurements, I then marked the ground to show the area of each of the forty-two pads that the engineer had confirmed would support the house.

Stuart Cameron arrived from the village with his digger and scooped out the soil for each hole (see appendices for dimensions). The surplus was used to build up a bank around the thousand gallon rainwater tank which was situated

down hill from the proposed building.

I then squared up the sides by hand and started to shift the local sandstone rubble by dumper truck across the field and up the woodland ride to the building site. After each hole was filled, I used a petrol piled wacker (compactor) to compact the stone and then laid a York stone slab on the top and compacted sand and stone around it. The York stone slabs had all come from people in the village, who after I had put the word out, found a few stones at the bottom of their gardens. I ended up with enough stone for all the foundation pads and some extra stone slabs for the fireplace.

Preparing the Cruck Frame

A regular sight throughout the summer was people working away with debarking spades and drawknives, removing grey brown chestnut bark to reveal the pure nakedness of the chestnut poles. The cruck poles were chosen from coppice stalls which have a 'swept butt'. When coppice is densely planted, the regrowth grows straight towards the light. When coppiced stools are spaced widely apart, the regrowth bends outwards before it grows upwards. This creates a slight arch ideal for cruck poles. Two poles are then joined together at the top and across the centre with a tie beam, and an A frame is formed.

Each cruck was laid out, measured and then jointed with a cup joint and pegged together. The cup joint ensures a snug contact between the two round-wood poles and ensures a heartwood to heartwood connection is made. On the cruck frames we used one inch diameter pegs. Drilling a hole to exactly one inch ensures a tight fit and the green wood of the cruck frame will then shrink tight onto the dry oak peg ensuring it is held firmly in place. As extra insurance that the peg will not move, oak wedges are then hammered into each end of the peg to expand the diameter.

Once the crucks were jointed together, we had to adjust the length at the base of the legs where they would sit upon the foundation pads. Although each padstone was set level, they were all at different levels to one another as we were building on a slope. A theodolite was therefore used to measure the differences in heights of the pads and the legs of the crucks were then cut accordingly. The four crucks were then stacked on top of one another ready for raising the following day.

Top Left:
Using a dumper to fill the foundation pad sites with local sandstone.

Centre Left:
All 42 pad sites had to be filled and compacted before finishing with a reclaimed York stone slab.

Bottom Left:
Poles laid out on the raising site.

Top:
An oak wedge being inserted into a round peg to stabilise the joint.

Above:
Considerable manpower was needed to manoeuvre the ridge pole into position prior to raising.

The Raise

There is a certain magic about the raising of a frame, the moment when all the preparation is put to the test and the skeleton of the house is lifted. Traditional raising was done by a large group of local people who happily came and helped raise the house of a fellow villager and in return knew there would be good food and drink to celebrate once the frame was up.

> Then he waved his arms and
> shouted "He-Oh-Heave! Lift...
> Till the sparks fly out of your eyes;
> it must go up: if it comes back it
> will kill the whole of us."

Building The Timber Frame House:
The Revival of a Forgotten Craft by Tedd Benson, 1980.

Most frame raising is now done by crane for safety reasons, although communities like the Amish in USA still raise in the traditional manner. For me it was a mixture of the modern and the traditional. I had a one point six tonne hand turfer winch to raise the frames, but also needed the help of friends.

The night before the raise I rang friends and neighbours, and eight of us were ready the following morning. Viv Goodings led the raising, his experience of rope work in raising marquees as well as his understanding of carpentry and building made him the perfect man for the job.

After a safety drill, we carried the thirty-two foot long ridgepole and secured it with ropes and ratchet straps to the first cruck to be raised. Each cruck had ropes attached so that once it was standing it could be supported by guy ropes anchored to chestnut stakes driven hard into the ground. Each cruck had a front and back line person, so one person let out the rope while the other took up the slack as the cruck began its journey from horizontal to vertical. The winch cable passed over an extra pair of chestnut legs to gain height so it lifted rather than dragged the cruck. I started to operate the ratchet on the winch, everyone was focused and the silence was only disturbed by tensioning ropes and cables and the creaking of the timber.

The first part of the lift is the most awkward as the cruck frame prefers to slide rather than pivot on its feet. Despite having the feet of the crucks tied down, they began to slide on the pad. The use of a couple of forestry cant hooks and some strong human energy ensured that the feet stayed put and the frame began to rise.

Slowly, inch by inch, the frame moved towards its upright position bringing the ridge pole up with it until it reached its finished place and the front and back lines were tied off. We checked the attached floor joists and found it to be exactly level, the theodolite does not lie.

The second cruck frame was more awkward, although we now had the extra height of the first cruck to give more leverage from the winch. We had to catch the hanging end of the ridgepole in the fork of the top of the second frame. Eventually we had to resort to using a long ladder to manoeuvre the cruck top into line with the ridgepole. By mid afternoon the second cruck was in place with ridgepole now pointing out horizontally in its finished position.

The third and fourth cruck frames went up very smoothly, with all of us involved now clear with the process and the hard work of positioning the ridge behind us. By early evening we were able to sit back and admire the four crucks and ridgepole standing up proudly in the woods. To me, at this stage, the frame looked very tall and narrow and resembled a giant frame in

Left:
Raising the frame. The crucks were laid out in position with the ridge pole on top. Then the first cruck was raised bringing the end of the ridge pole with it. Eventually all four crucks *were raised and the first stage of the build was complete.*

Above:
Cant hooks and manpower help stabilise a frame during the raise.

which fairground swing boats could hang. The amount of rope securing the frame in position gave it a slightly nautical feel, a feeling that stayed with the house as it evolved and is still very apparent in its finished state.

Now was the time for celebration. I brought out a gallon of my homemade cider, and we then proceeded to a local hostelry, where drinking and feasting carried on into the early hours.

The next stage was to start to tie all the frames together. Two thirty-two foot chestnut poles were jointed onto the four curving feet of the crucks and pegged to form support for the floor joists. A separate central support was positioned on a series of tenoned chestnut 'saddle stones', which in turn sat on York stone pads. The eight wall posts were then jointed and temporarily strapped into position. Their role was to carry the wall plate and to 'pick up' the tie beams while being jointed at the base to the foot of the crucks.

Before the pegs were hammered home, four concave braces were tenoned into the end cruck, forming the bracing between the crucks and the wall posts. The wall posts were then drawn into the concave brace to locate their final position and all the pegs were hammered home.

Lifting the two thirty-two foot wall plates onto the top of the wall posts was a four person activity. Then the wall plates were scribed and mortises chiselled out and the tenon on the top of each of the wall posts was formed. Two convex braces (wind braces) were positioned on each side from the wall posts to the wall plate. The frame at this stage was still attached by ropes and had a large amount of movement.

I went searching in the woods for four matching cross braces to cross between the middle crucks. They looked like long alpine horns and were tenoned into the crucks. These braces form a major part of the racking on the building, stopping lateral movement. Towards the end of the build Spike appeared and tied them together at the centre with rope, again adding to the nautical feel of the building. The end and middle crucks were tied together further with a horizontal tie and jointed to the cruck pole and tie beam of each cruck frame. The roundwood upper floor joists were cup jointed into position and day-by-day the rocking movement of the building was quelled.

Later I decided to secure the house to the ground with earth anchors. Although not asked for by building control or suggested by the engineers, I know the strength of the winter winds and felt I would sleep more soundly knowing the house was firmly anchored to the ground.

The Roof

The roof was formed primarily by six inch by two inch rafters. I had mobile milled these in the woods the previous winter. They were secured to the ridge and wall plates using five inch annular ringed stainless steel nails. The rafters were positioned at six hundred millimetre centres. Once the rafters passed the wall plate, chestnut sprocketed ends were attached to give the roof its characterful shape and slow down the run-off water to the gutters.

The four visible rafters at the gable ends of the building were sweet chestnut, carefully selected with a swept butt so they had a straight run to match the larch, and sprocketed ends to match the curves of the other rafters all flowing in one piece of wood. The large

Top Left:
The model of the house sits beside the erected cruck frame. Note the cross braces fitted between the middle crucks which help prevent the frame from racking.

Bottom Left:
Earth anchors were used to secure the frame to the ground.

Above:
Aligning a post to the frame.

rafters were doubled up and noggins attached to allow for the positioning of roof windows. A breathable waterproof membrane was then battened on using one inch by one and a half inch larch battens. Counter battens were put in place using one and a half by one inch battens in preparation for the shingles.

The shingles or shakes were sweet chestnut and the main roof used ten thousand with another two thousand for the main veranda roof which was added later. Each shingle was pre-drilled and attached with a single copper clout nail, two nails being used on the outside shingles. To save on cost scaffolding was kept to a minimum which meant using harnesses and ropes anchored to the main floor support beams.

This was all very well in theory but the morning we were due to begin shingling, the work force was small and none of us had sufficient experience to set up a range of safe rope access lines. While we were sitting around the fire discussing how to proceed, Tom from Bradford appeared. He had come to volunteer on the build. When I asked him whether he had had much experience with ropes, to my delight he revealed that he was a rock climbing instructor. It wasn't long before the three of us were hanging off ropes fixing shingles.

Shingling happened during a short heatwave. I remember long days working from 5:30am until 8:30 at night as the sun beat down on us and the beautiful texture of the scale-like wooden roof moved like the sun's shadow across the battens. The ridge was sealed with a dressed piece of copper sheeting beaten into place and drilled and copper nailed. All the nail heads were subsequently soldered over to ensure that it was totally watertight.

I also used copper for all the guttering and downpipes.

The Lean-to Frames

We had erected a framing tent, a large open area with a canvas roof and had laid out some large rafters to form a level bed from which to work. All five lean-to frames were colour coded to ensure there was no mix up of poles. Each frame was drawn out on a blackboard showing the position of mortise and tenon joints and the lengths of each section to the millimetre, calculated by the theodolite measurements.

Jointing together a roundwood frame is challenging but wonderfully satisfying as the poles do not have to be totally straight. First one examines the pole to find the most even plane and then marks out a centre with a string line. The position for mortises is then worked to a flat face in the heartwood using a hand adze and drawknife, the string line ensuring the mortises are centred in the same plane. The mortises were cut with very large framing chisels and a one inch corner chisel. Tenons were cut with a Japanese saw and chisels, and the frame was fitted together in the tent. Once completed, all measurements were checked and re-checked and triangulation measurements were also checked to ensure that, although made of roundwood, the frame was 'in square'.

After this, all the components of the frame were thoroughly marked as it was disassembled and then re-assembled in its raising position with its feet on the stone pads. Temporary bracing was nailed across the frame to avoid it twisting and the raising was achieved with winch and ropes and usually a minimum of four people. This was with the exception of the long and heavy veranda frame which took eight of us to lift into place.

Some frames were totally constructed by a pair of volunteers working as a team, whereas others were made up by

Top Left:
Shingling the lower part of the main roof.
Note the sprocketed curve at the eaves.

Centre Left:
Ropes and harnesses in use.

Bottom Left:
The texture of the completed roof.

Top:
Raising the main veranda frame.
Frames like this were made by a small team in a framing tent and then moved to their final position.

Bottom:
A proud frame building team with the lean-to section they made.

roofs because they were at too shallow an angle to use shingles. Onduline is corrugated fibreboard and has a great degree of flexibility. Where the Onduline covered the port outside the kitchen door, I used chestnut rafters and one inch chestnut rounds fixed tightly together so that when looking up, the appearance of the light colour of the chestnut peeled rafters would contrast with the dark of the chestnut bark on the one inch rounds. The corrugated Onduline would not be visible.

The main veranda lean-to roof was constructed differently. This was formed

a flow of different people who might do one mortise or tenon. All the frames were completed, raised and fitted without problems, a testament to the importance of overseeing the continuity of each frame, whoever was working on it.

The lean-to roofs were constructed with six inch by two inch rafters as in the main roof. The Klober Permoforte breathable membrane was battened to the rafters and then Onduline panels were secured onto two inch by two inch support rafters. Onduline seemed to be the best and the most economical solution to the pitch of the lean-to

using three inch sweet chestnut round rafters with round chestnut battens that increased in diameter as they ascended up the rafters. This increased the roof pitch to allow for shingling.

It was important to me that this roof was shingled as the house is on a slope and, when viewed from the western aspect, one is standing up hill from the house and the veranda roof is immediately visible. The effect of the roundwood rafters and battens also gives a lovely feeling when sitting on the veranda looking up at the hand picked timbers whilst enjoying the afternoon sun.

The Floor

The floor was constructed in two parts. The first, the lower floor, consisted of panel vent (a non-toxic particle board). This was attached to the underside of the six inch by two inch larch floor joists. The second was made from kiln-dried tongue and grooved oak. We used floor clamps and secret pinned the floorboards by pre-drilling and then fixing cheridised lost head nails through the tongue on each board. The floor went down in about three days and the house had an almost Japanese feel as we stood on freshly laid wooden boards looking out across the green of the woodland with no walls, just a floor and roof, raised up off the ground.

The floorboards adjacent to the edges of the house were left unattached to allow for insulation to be blown in.

Top Left:
A lovely contrast – the light colour of the rafters set against the darkness of unpeeled chestnut rods above.

Centre Left:
Working on the veranda roof. Note the copper ridge on the main roof.

Bottom Left:
Onduline roofing which is made from bitumin saturated organic fibres.

Above:
Laying the tongued and grooved oak flooring which was all secret nailed.

Right:
The sunlight streaming into the open sided structure. Not having walls at this stage gave it quite a tropical feel.

Insulation

My preference for insulation was to use sheep's wool. I have worked as a shepherd at different times of my life and know sheep's wool to be the most wonderful natural warm material. It is perfect for insulation. Wool does not burn, it just singes and goes out, and in our present agricultural climate any markets for wool are more than welcome. To use the wool for insulation on this build, however, meant the wool had to meet standards set by building regulations. This has limited the number of companies supplying wool and their prices have put wool insulation out of the reach of a large proportion of the population. Today, I am glad to report that I have recently used sheep's wool in another building I have completed and the price had come down to a more affordable level.

In the end, I opted for Warmcell for the Woodland House, a fire proofed recycled paper option which is blown into the cavity between the two floors and also between the ceiling and the roof. It is quick to install and the whole house, floors and roof were insulated in one very long day.

Windows

The windows had been made to bale sizes and I screwed them into the larch buck frames incorporated into the studwork. The glazing had been ordered from a local glass firm and consisted of double glazed units of four/twelve/four; four millimetres of glass, twelve millimetre air gap and four millimetres of glass. This was satisfactory for building regulations at the time although since my build, the regulations require a higher grade of double-glazing. The glass was fitted with a double-sided glass tape, a special glass sealing silicone and then beaded with six millimetres of ash.

Straw

Keeping bales dry before, during and after the build, is the essential part to straw bale building. The bales I purchased had been stored in a barn, and were then transported by tractor and trailer on a dry day, stacked on pallets and covered with well-secured tarpaulins. They were then moved onto the oak floor as soon as it was in place. The bale stack was therefore in the centre of the house, ideal for dismantling as we built up the

walls all around it.

Before building the walls, metal spikes with a flat plate were coach screwed into the floor joists, ensuring a very strong and rigid foundation for the bottom level of bales. The floors were a minimum of eighteen inches above the ground, so the bales were well clear of rising moisture.

After the first layer of bales were in place, the others followed in a traditional bricklaying pattern, using chestnut stakes hammered through each layer to secure and stabilise the wall. Bales were built up to a sawn larch box or 'buck' frame into which the windows were inserted. The two inch larch studwork frame was constructed around the outside of the

Top Left:
The floor with crucks 'growing' out of it.

Centre Left:
Warmcell being blown into the roof.

Bottom Left:
Loading the insulation blower.

Top:
Main frame, lean to and studwork.

Centre:
Window frames and larch studwork.

Left:
Straw bale wall showing bale spikes.

bales to give stability and to facilitate the attachment of the oak and chestnut weatherboarding. Bales were customised using bale needles. These allowed for two pieces of baler twine to pass through the bale and be re-tied when needed. Then the original strings could be cut and smaller sections of bales could be perfectly formed for awkward corners and around the windows.

Above the buck frame of the windows, a wooden lintel and chicken wire mesh was created stuffed with straw and curved to create an aesthetically pleasing soft curve above the windows. Elsewhere I trimmed bales with a chainsaw and cut interesting niches for candles or ornaments with an angle grinder and arbotech blade. The trimming with the chainsaw gave the bales a neat but rough finish, ideal for keying in the first layer of plaster.

Building with bales is a fun and satisfying process. Everyone involved is always amazed at the speed a bale wall is constructed. Provided the dimensions of the house are worked to the bale sizes, walls can go up very fast. It is only when bales need re-sizing or lintels need re-forming that the process is slowed down.

Everyone was keen to bale build and I have fond memories of dusty straw faces with beaming smiles in the midst of the summer heat. A word of warning though, this is probably the most likely time for a fire accident to occur. It is essential that loose straw is swept up and bagged and removed from the building at least once a day. The loose straw can be used in the making of earth plasters at a later time.

Weatherboard

A breathable membrane was used prior to fitting the weatherboard as this gave an extra insulative and waterproof layer without compromising the building's ability to breathe. I used Klober Permaforte.

The weatherboard was a mixture of waney edged oak and chestnut that I had milled up with a mobile mill prior to beginning the build.

The key points with waney edge boards, especially oak, is to make sure there is a good overlap of heartwood from board to board as sap wood would perish and fall away. Waney edge board is traditionally fixed onto uprights on the building with intermediate supports. Having made roundwood frames, I wanted to see the frames exposed. I therefore needed stud work between the roundwood chestnut uprights to get a fixing for the waney edge boards. But by using roundwood, the posts are not straight and each board needs to be scribed and cut with a jigsaw so that it butted up tight to the roundwood posts. This at least trebled the time it would normally have taken to board out a building, but to me the result made it all worthwhile. The unusual character of the round poles stayed visible and the house maintained its rustic charm.

Remember boards will shrink; try and at least semi-season boards before fixing and always pre-drill before nailing.

Top Left:
Tying straw bales in the kitchen area. Note the wattle internal wall and the restored Rayburn on left.

Bottom Left:
A chainsaw trimmed bale wall ready for plastering.

Above:
Waney edged weather boarding. Every piece had to be measured and cut to fit between the roundwood frames.

Left:
Weather boarding and a small double glazed window.

PLASTERING AND SERVICES

The Rayburn

Plastering

Lime

Clay

The Fireplace

Electrics

Hot Water

Reedbed & Compost Toilet

Chapter Six

Ultramarine blue limewash on the compost toilet wall.

The Rayburn

The Rayburn is a solid fuel hob, oven, water heater and wood burner all in one classically cast piece. I obtained mine from some friends who had a reconditioned 'Rayburn Royale' in pieces getting dusty in their greenhouse. The Rayburn sits in the kitchen and has a character of its own. It can be rather moody when strong easterly winds rip across the fields towards the house and it has a mind of its own when you want to get the oven really hot. Some days it races up to 250 degrees centigrade in less than half an hour after lighting, while on others, despite coaxing it with finely chopped pieces of well seasoned ash, it stays around 160 degrees centigrade for hours. What it does very efficiently is to supply regular tanks of piping hot water. The highlight of its excellent design is a 'bum bar', the rail along the front which is perfect for drying clothes or just to lean against when you come in from working in the cold.

It was installed early in the building process and proved very useful during the plastering stage.

Plastering

I chose to use both lime and earth plasters in the construction of the house. Both have good and bad points as the table below shows:

Properties of Lime and Earth Plasters

	To Apply	Insulation Value	Exposure to Weather	Vermin Proof
Lime	Poor	Good	Good	Good
Earth	Very Good	Very Good	Poor	Poor

Lime Plaster

I chose lime plaster for the straw bale walls. First I chainsawed the edge of the bales to create a rough textured finish and then mixed a hurling coat of three to one mix of sharp sand and lime putty and added a lot of water to the mix to create a sloppy mixture with the consistency of a thick custard. This I then applied with a hurling trowel and quite literally flicked the mixture so it splattered against the bales. It didn't take me long to realise that this was a messy process and I paused to wrap plastic around all the exposed woodwork, the floor was already covered with tarpaulin.

The hurling coat left a dappled pattern of lime across the bale walls and, once it was set, I trowelled on a thick three to one coat of sharp sand

and lime putty with horse and cow hair mixed in. This was hand trowelled and bonded well to the bale walls.

It was already late October, so there was not any worry of the lime drying out too fast and cracking, as can be the case in the summer if it isn't draped with damp Hessian sheeting. It was in fact the opposite and I lit the Rayburn to try and speed up the drying out process. Once the haired coat had begun to go off, I used a scratch comb to make ripples in the plaster so that it would create a textured surface to make a firm bond with the third coat.

After this coat, I mist sprayed the walls and added the third coat, the finishing coat. Again it was a three-to-one sharp sand and lime putty but without the added hair. This was trowelled on and once it had begun to go off, I finished it with a damp sponge. I created a natural textured feel that went with the lack of straight lines in the house by dragging the sponge gently down the plaster. This also helped to hide the fact that I am not over proficient with a finishing trowel!

Once the plaster had gone off I applied coats of lime wash by brush to the walls. I used natural pigments such as yellow ochre and iron oxide to create colours in the lime wash and had some fun experimenting with the spice cupboard which meant one room was coloured with a mixture of turmeric and iron oxide.

A word of warning, lime is a wonderful plaster as it breathes, is weatherproof and is also acts as a rodenticide, keeping mice away, but is unpleasant to apply and will burn if it makes contact with your skin. This means wearing overalls, gloves and goggles at all times during plastering or lime washing.

Top Left:
Ben applying lime plaster around a straw bale window opening.

Above:
Clay plaster on chestnut lathes. This was used on all internal walls.

The Fireplace

I based the design of my fireplace on the work of Count Rumford, who lived in the eighteenth century. The Count is primarily known for the work he did on the nature of heat. He wrote two essays detailing his improvements on fireplaces in 1795 and 1798 and, until coal became favoured over wood, his design was used worldwide.

He felt that fireplaces were too large and that they wasted too much heat up the chimney and pulled too much cold air into the room. He also worked out from his studies of heat that if a fireplace is shallow, preferably one third as deep as it is wide, and the sides are angled to a maximum of one hundred and thirty five degrees to the back of the fire box, more heat would be reflected into the room.

Rumford rounded off the front of the firebox in his design so smoke from the fire is able to follow its natural pattern going up the chimney without hindrance. His design for a throat opening includes the use of a damper which leaves the chimney open. This can be reduced in a similar way to a wood burning stove and allows for a slower burning of wood, but with maximum heat radiation into the room. Another benefit of the straight back of the firebox and the rounded or

Clay Plaster

A clay based earth plaster is a pleasure to use after lime. There is no need for goggles or gloves, even the plastering trowel can be chucked aside and the clay plaster can be moulded against the split chestnut lathe with your hands. I have always liked getting my hands dirty so burying my hands into a sticky clay plaster and slapping it onto the wall is pure pleasure.

There are many different thoughts and recipes for what makes a good earth plaster but I have always felt it is dependent on knowing your soil. The clay I was using came from a seam that had been successfully used to make bricks and I had also used it to make clay ovens. I therefore knew its qualities and was able to proportion my mix based on that information. I used two parts clay to one part sand and a few large handfuls of chopped straw to make a plasterers bath full of mixture. This was then mixed with water to make a thick malleable mixture.

I had always mixed my earth plasters with a shovel but it was Mark (who had been working with cob buildings in America) who introduced me to the bare foot method with the use of a tarpaulin to do the turning rather than labouring with a shovel. Despite the fact

it was well into autumn and the water was cold from the spring, there was always someone who was willing to hoist up their trousers and get that feeling of clay between their toes.

Once the plaster had dried, some cracking naturally appeared and I then applied a slip coat or two of a pure clay and water mixture to a consistency of a thick soup. This is again applied by hand and rubbed over the last coat of plaster, making sure to push more into any large cracks. After a couple of coats the cracking totally vanished and a lovely warm earthy wall remained.

streamline throat is that the smoke is kept hotter further up the chimney. This keeps a cleaner burn. Under laboratory conditions the design has met USA wood burning appliance emission regulations.

As I write, I am sitting in front of the hot Rumford fireplace on a March evening and there is snow beginning to settle on the ground. The Rayburn and Rumford stove are the only forms of heating in the house, but with good insulation, I am cosy and warm tonight.

I built the fireplace using a stone clay foundation with a large York stone slab as a plinth. I built a pipe through the floor to the base of the firebox to allow a controlled draw of outside air needed for the fire. The firebox itself is constructed from secondhand firebricks from a night storage heater. I cut the bricks in half with an angle grinder and then fire cemented them into place. This has given a rough finish and it now looks like natural stone as it is darkened from a couple of years of open fires.

The angle of the sides, the depth of the box and the height of the opening are all based on Rumford figures for a twenty-four inch fireplace. The rounded throat is made from pre-cast clay and a steel damper has been fitted. This then continues into a pre-cast clay smoke chamber and then into an eight inch double insulated steel flue pipe.

I built up around the firebox and throat with clay and constructed a chestnut and chicken wire frame over which I plastered a clay earth plaster. I rounded the entrance to the firebox by creating a rolled piece of chicken wire filled with crushed firebrick. This was covered with an earth plaster which softened all the edges and created an adobe type appearance.

The fireplace is so much the heart of the house and I wanted a natural look without compromising good energy

Top Left:
Finished clay plaster internal wall. Note the roundwood door frame.

Bottom Left:
1) Rumford fireplace, firebox made from reused firebricks, throat and smoke chamber.

2) Stainless steel double insulated flue with shaped chicken-wire frame ready for plastering.

Above:
The very natural looking finished Rumford fireplace. Both efficient and aesthetically pleasing.

on twelve volt DC rather than invert it to two hundred and forty volts AC. This is because I am used to living with twelve volts DC and have many items of equipment, such as a stereo, lights and laptop, designed to run off twelve-volt direct current. Inversion to two hundred and forty volts AC loses some power in the process and I wanted to keep all the power I had. But the main reason for keeping twelve volt DC is that as far as I know, no one has ever died from twelve volt DC. It is for me a safer current to be dealing with in an off-the-grid situation such as mine.

efficiency. I believe I have achieved my aim. Comments from visitors have included, "It looks like a tree growing up through the house". If I can make the fireplace resemble a tree, then I am a long way to creating a house that blends in with the woodland.

Electrics

Prior to the build, I lived with a small amount of twelve-volt direct current solar and wind power. This was enough for my basic needs of living in a caravan with a few lights, a stereo and a laptop computer. The house was a bigger

proposition and I needed a larger array of solar panels and some good brains to help me design the system. For this I turned to two good friends, James Berrow, an experienced electrician, and Howard Johns of Southern Solar, who fits a lot of photovoltaic systems.

I already had a large battery bank that consists of six two volt ex-submarine batteries with a capacity of nine hundred and twenty amp hours. In simple terms, this means I have a large capacity to store a lot of electricity to make up for the times when there may not be much sun or wind. I wanted to keep the house

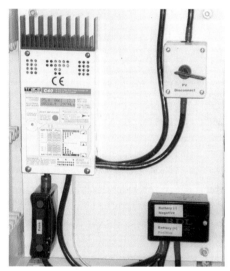

Having decided on a twelve volt system, James ran a series of calculations to work out the sizes of cable needed to ensure that every light fitting and power point received a full twelve volt DC. One of the major disadvantages of twelve volt DC is that voltage drops away over the distance it is carried. If there is twelve volt DC in the battery and the lights you wish to power are ten metres away, there will be a loss of voltage between the two unless the cable is large enough to compensate for the voltage drop. James not only calculated all the cable sizes, he also recommended

I used mineral cable. This was to ensure that the cables running through the straw bales were rodent proof and there would be no risk of electrical fire. Mineral cable is a cable coated in copper and mice are unable to penetrate it.

I already had a couple of Rutland wind generators, a 913 and a standard, both of which produced small amounts of power in low wind speeds. I also had an Air four 400. This is a wind generator that needs a higher wind speed to start generating but it can produce up to four hundred watts once it is turning.

Howard managed to get me a very good deal on photovoltaic cells and I acquired some hardly used panels (courtesy of Big Brother House). These give me a 500 watt (half a kilowatt) system. Again one of the key factors in setting up solar panels and wind turbines is ensuring that the cables are correct so

that there is no loss between the panel, the turbine and the batteries. Howard used a multicore cable connected to the batteries via a Trace charge controller. This important devise tells me through a digital read out the current (amps) coming in from the solar panels to the batteries, the voltage of the batteries and the amount of amp hours generated. It also has a shut down mechanism which can be set to a chosen voltage which will shut down the solar panels when the batteries are totally full. It is, in my experience, a very worthwhile piece of equipment.

So what can my system power? November and December are the worst power months for me, as the sun is low and rare and the evenings long and dark. I run only lights and a stereo at this time and make use of other equipment as the nights draw out.

At my house warming party, the system comfortably supported a six-piece band. I have also run projected DVD cinema evenings without any power difficulties. As with any off the grid system, it is all about monitoring the battery voltage and adapting to the weather conditions. If there is a week of grey, still days it is probably best to go to bed early.

Top Left:
AIR 400 wind generator.

Centre Left:
Trace 12 volt charge controller.

Bottom Left:
Six 2 volt ex-submarine batteries storing 920 amp hours.

Above:
0.5 kilowatt photovoltaic array.

Hot Water

Hot water is generated by a back boiler on the wood fired Rayburn which more than adequately heats the water in winter. In summer, it is generated by a solar panel. The panel is an Imagination Solar low flow system. The system involves having a twin coiled hot water cylinder with one coil from the Rayburn and one from the solar panel. Collected rainwater is pumped by twelve volt to a header tank in the roof and this then creates a gravity pressure feed to the hot water cylinder. Winter baths are a joy after a hard working day in the woods. Most winter days the water is between ninety and one hundred degrees so a hot bath is guaranteed!

Reed Bed and Compost Toilet

All wastewater from baths, shower and sinks runs through a series of four reed beds and then emerges into a small pond from where it flows through a willow planting and then onto another pond. The reed beds filter the water as the roots of the plants feed on the grey or wastewater, cleaning the water more as it passes through each individual bed. No sewage passes through the system as human waste is composted in a dry composting toilet. The toilet is sited in the northeast corner of the house away from direct sunlight and, with the house being on stilts, the collecting chamber is under the house and can be emptied from outside. The gap between the seat and chamber is spanned by a series of highly adjustable 'manhole risers', which form an air tight seal. The chamber is emptied about every three months and is then composted further in a heap. The finished compost is spread around the fruit trees. Sawdust, ash from the fire and charcoal fines are added to the chamber after each use.

Top Left:
The solar panel that provides much of the hot water. Because the house has no south facing roof slope the panel was sited on the ground

Bottom Left:
Dry composting toilet. It is emptied from underneath the house

Above:
The woodland house bathed in sunshine with Oilly making the most of the warmth of the south facing deck.

Right:
The house and its three wind turbines viewed from the NE, with the woods rising up behind it.

REFLECTIONS
Building With Volunteers
Two Years On

Chapter Seven

Two volunteers taking a break from plastering.

Building With Volunteers

Building with volunteers is both a challenging and rewarding process if you can get the 'mix' just right. As I said, volunteers are giving free labour, enthusiasm, and a different perspective and hope in return to gain knowledge, skills and have an enjoyable time. I had ninety six volunteers pass through during the build from all over the globe and ended up making many new friends. I feel enriched from the whole experience. I hope the volunteers left with a similar feeling, having enjoyed good food, good company and learnt a few skills.

At times I had just a couple of volunteers and at others up to twelve at once. It takes a lot of focus. As the build manager you have to have enough activities up your sleeve to keep everyone busy but you also have to ensure activities are being done to a satisfactory standard. I think, overall, I managed this quite well. The summer passed by and a building appeared amidst laughter and music. The final month was the hardest for me and by the time I was plastering, I was tired and ready to slow down for the winter.

My sense of humour began to wane and at that stage I can't have been the easiest of build managers.

It was the enthusiasm of volunteers, people who wanted to be involved in the build and believe that there are other ways of building that literally 'do not cost the earth', that made my house appear on the landscape. I hope they gained some useful skills and fond memories from the experience. You know who you are: *Thank you.*

Two Years On

I have now been living in my house for two years and it has become my home, or rather our home. I live here with Bev, my wife, and feel proud that our home is a low impact dwelling.

The quality of the structure and it's insulation ensures we are warm and cosy during the winter, but the fact that the house relies totally on firewood for its heating means that in terms of routine little has changed, it's still 'chop wood to

keep warm and cook the dinner'.

The experience of 'living within one's dream' is continually nourishing. Often I will look in detail at one part of the house and remember a day or a person and a whole host of memories come flooding back; few houses come with this feature! The process of filming the house ensured a record of the build was kept and is a lovely memento of a major milestone in my life. The importance of the *Grand Designs* programme was to show others that we can build sustainable houses that are both cheap and beautiful. A friend of mine described the programme as 'touching the psyche of the nation'. It also showed that there are many people wanting to live a simple life, in touch with their environment.

I am sure a time will come, if not in my lifetime then certainly in my children's, when after we have greedily depleted the earth of it's oil resources, structures like the woodland house will have come of age. Some people will work with those around them and the materials of their locality to build beautiful structures with room for individual artistic creativity, and our world will be a better place for it.

People ask me whether living in a house means that I have lost 'connection' with the woodland way of life. For me, my life has become more comfortable, and I hope this will ensure a longer life and that I will be able to see my days out in the woods. My connection with the woods, the symbiotic relationship of working the coppice and living within it, are far stronger today than when I built my first 'bender'. My connection with the land continues to grow as Bev and I are managing the surrounding pasture with a flock of Jacob sheep, breeding our own meat. As we develop our woodland garden, full of produce and beauty, the 'woodland way' expands and further unfolds.

Top Left:
Two of the ninety six volunteers who helped make the build such a success.

Bottom Left:
Wide site view of the completed project and some of the Jacob sheep.

Top:
The house after two years, enhanced by the addition of a southern deck.

Above:
View from the west showing the large veranda.

Top Left:
The completed house with chestnut product garden.

Bottom Left:
Planting on and around the oak boarded veranda.

Above:
The use of roundwood chestnut links the house and garden together.

Right:
Sculptural garden gate with the southern veranda beyond.

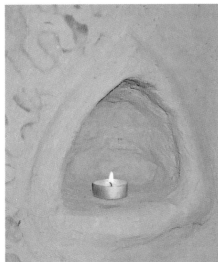

Top Left:
1) Bathroom detail and view.
2) Dining area and library.

Bottom Left:
Part of the kitchen.

Above:
Candle light fittings.

Right:
Kitchen window seat.

Top Left:
Living room and fireplace.

Bottom Left:
Dining area and oak door to bedroom.

Top:
Rope binding on the bracing struts.

Centre:
Sculpted reveal around gable light.

Right:
Looking across the central well.

APPENDICES

Appendices

Looking up at the main veranda roof.

About the Author

Ben has always colonised the edge of society. He was educated at six different schools, due to family moves and personal expulsion. He left school at 15 and worked on a smallholding, growing fruit and vegetables and looking after livestock. He spent a year at Sparsholt College where he gained an Advanced National Certificate in Agriculture and then continued working as a shepherd and set up a conservation landscaping business, specialising in ponds and wild flower meadows. Woodlands were a natural progression and after seeking out a few experienced coppice workers, he began work in the woods and in associated coppice crafts.

Ben visited the Amazon in the late 1980s looking for positive solutions to deforestation and on his return set up and directed the charity, The Forest Management Foundation, working primarily with community forestry in Papua New Guinea and was a founding member of the Forest Stewardship Council. The bureaucracy of international forest policy and a realisation that true sustainability begins at home, resulted in his returning to the coppice woods of West Sussex to become a forest dweller. He has lived and worked at Prickly Nut Wood for 14 years, and trains apprentices and runs courses on sustainable woodland management and permaculture design. Ben helped set up and chaired the Sussex and Surrey Coppice group and also worked for Oxfam as a permaculture consultant in Albania.

He is the author of *The Woodland Way, a permaculture approach to sustainable woodland management* and set a precedent in planning law by achieving permission to build his woodland house. The building of his house was filmed for Channel 4's *Grand Designs* and proved to be the most popular programme of the series. He lives with his wife Bev and is happiest when he is working on the land.

Acknowledgements

Building the woodland house must be the goal of every woodland worker and caretaker of our forests. For me it has been the practical pleasure of turning a dream into reality. Undertaking a project of this size and unusual complexity takes many people and my thanks go out to the 96 volunteers who helped make this happen in seven months. In particular, I would like to thank the core workers: Julie, Andrew, Tim, Viv, John, Tom, Adrian, Anis, Phil, James, Steve, Howard... the list goes on. I would like to thank Steve Morley for his photographic documentation of the project, some of which is displayed in this book, and to Sarah Morley for transcribing my verbal ramblings into a workable first draft. A special thank you goes to John Rees of Constructive Individuals who was a constant support throughout the project and stayed calm while I struggled with the frustrations of bureaucracy. To my family who have supported me throughout, acknowledging my need and desire to live the woodland way. To the *Grand Designs* team and the folk at *Talkback* for their professional approach. To my publishers, Tim and Maddy Harland and the team at *Permanent Publications*, for protecting my privacy. To my dog Oilly for always being pleased to see me. Lastly, to my wife Bev for helping to turn the woodland house into our home.

Appendix II

Glossary

Adze: An axe-like tool with its blade at right angles to its handle, used to shape or dress timbers.

Bender: Temporary home or shelter made from hazel branches and canvas covering, used commonly in woodlands.

Cant hook: Forestry hand tool based on leverage enables the moving of large timbers.

Cleave: To split unsawn timber by forcing the fibres apart along its length.

Clout nails: nails with large heads used primarily for roofing.

Coppice: Broadleaf trees cut during the dormant season which produce continual multi-stems that are harvested for wood products.

Corner chisel: A heavy duty L-shaped chisel struck with a mallet. Used for cutting or cleaning out corners of a mortice.

Cruck: Primitive truss formed by two main timbers, usually curved, set up as an arch or inverted V.

Draw knife: A knife blade with handles on both ends so that the knife can be pulled by both hands towards the user.

Framing chisel: A heavy-duty chisel, often with wide blade. Designed to be struck with a mallet.

Greenwood: Freshly cut wood.

Joist: Parallel timbers that make up the floor frame onto which floor boards are attached.

Lath: Thin narrow strips of wood, usually cleaved from roundwood and used with plaster in walls and ceilings.

Mortise: A slot into which or through a tenon is inserted.

Mortise and Tenon Joint: A joint in which a projection on one end of a timber is inserted into a slot in another timber.

Noggin (Nogs, Noggings): Short lengths of timber fixed at 90 degrees between adjacent roof rafters or floor joists.

Permaculture: An ecological design system to create a sustainable future.

Ridgepole: A horizontal timber at the peak of the roof to which the rafters are attached.

Scarf Joint: A joint for splicing together two timbers, end to end.

Scribe: To mark a timber by scratching a line and also to shape a timber so that it fits the irregular surface of another timber.

Shaving Horse: A quick release clamp for holding wood on which the woodworker sits; a foot-operated swinging arm acts as the clamp.

Sprocket: Short piece of wood that is attached to the lower end of the roof rafters to extend the roof further over the wall. The angle of the sprocket is usually less than the main roof to slow down water run-off.

Tenon: The projecting end of a timber that is inserted into a mortise.

Tie-beam: A beam that spans the width of a building from wall plate to wall plate.

Wall Plate: A timber that runs horizontally along the top of the wall onto which the rafters are attached.

Yurt: A wooden framed transportable dwelling with canvas cover originating from Asia and now often found as a dwelling in woodlands.

Further Reading

Building The Timber Frame House[†]; Benson, Tedd (1995); Fireside.
ISBN 0 684 17286 0
Excellent American frame publication. Full of plans, jointing techniques and engineering formula.

Build It With Bales[†]; Myhrman, MA and SO Macdonald (1997); Chelsea Green.
ISBN 0 9642821 19
Still the most practical bale building guide available.

Building With Straw Bales[†]; Jones, B (2002); Green Books.
ISBN 1 903998 13 1
Guide for UK climate by one of Britain's leading bale builders.

Digest 445, Building Research Establishment (2000); CRC Ltd.
ISBN 1 86081 378 X
Stress grading calculations for sweet chestnut.

The Earth Care Manual – A Permaculture Handbook For Britain And Other Temperate Climates[†]; Whitefield, Patrick (2004); Permanent Publications.
ISBN: 1 85623 021 X
Meticulously researched, informative and highly readable.

Energy Efficient Building – The Best Of Fine Homebuilding[†]; (1999); Taunton Press.
ISBN 1 56158 340 5
Excellent collection of articles, I was inspired by the Kiva fireplace.

The Green Building Bible[†]; editor Hall, Keith (2005); Green Building Press.
ISBN 1 89813 002 7
Essential information for ecobuilding, includes a list of AECB members.

Green Building Handbook, Volume 1[†]; Woolley T, S Kimmins, R Harrison and P Harrison (1997); Spon Press.
ISBN: 0 41922 690 7
Compares the environmental effects of different building materials.

Green Building Handbook, Volume 2[†]; Woolley T and S Kimmins (2000); Spon Press.
ISBN: 0 41925 380 7
Companion to Vol. 1 but with emphasis on wiring, glazing, adhesives and ventilation.

Low-Cost Pole Building Construction[†]; Wolfe, Ralph (1980); Storey Publishing.
ISBN 0 88266 170 1
Some useful pole building designs and possible jointing options.

Appendix IV

The Natural Plaster Book[†]; Guelberth, CR, and D Chiras (2003); New Society.
ISBN 0 86571 449 5
Earth, lime and gypsum plasters explained.

A Pattern Language[†]; Alexander, Christopher, Sara Ishikawa and Silverstein Murray (1977); Oxford University Press.
ISBN: 0 19501 919 1
Essential read prior to designing any living space.

Permaculture – A Designer's Manual; Mollison, Bill (1988); Tagari Publications.
ISBN: 0 90822 801 5
The original manual that started me on this path.

Places Of The Soul[†]; Day, Christopher (1990); Harper Collins.
ISBN 1 85538 305 5
Inspirational angle on architecture. The antidote to 'Sick Building Syndrome.'

Serious Straw Bale[†]; Lacinski, P and M Bergeron (2000); Chelsea Green.
ISBN 1 890132 64 0
Best section on moisture in straw bale houses that I have come across.

The Straw Bale House[†]; Steen, AS, D Bainbridge and B Steen (1994); Chelsea Green.
ISBN 0 930031 71 7
Good pictures and some good designs.

Timber Building in Britain[†]; Brunskill RW (1990); Gollancz.
ISBN 0 575 06735 7
The history of Britain's timber framing heritage. Excellent framing glossary.

Timber Frame Construction[†]; Sobon, Jack and Roger Schroeder (1984); Storey Publishing.
ISBN 0 88266 365 8
Good all round framing book.

Timber Pole Construction[†]; Jayanetti, Lionel (1990); Intermediate Technology Publications. ISBN 1 85339 068 2
Basic and practical as you would expect from I.T.

The Woodland Way[†]; Law, Ben (2001); Permanent Publications.
ISBN: 1 85623 009 0
The way of life that led to the building of the house.

Titles marked [†] are available from *Permaculture Magazine's Earth Repair Catalogue*. Contact: Permanent Publications, The Sustainability Centre, East Meon, Hampshire GU32 1HR. Tel: 0845 458 4150 (local rate), +44 1730 823 311 (international), Fax: 01730 823 322 or order online at our website: www.permaculture.co.uk

Resources

A&F Warehouse
Unit 13, Hurstfold Farm, Fernhurst, West Sussex GU27 3JG
Tel: 01428 661 767
Web: www.afwarehouse.co.uk
Forestry harnesses, rope access equipment, chainsaws

Ben Law
C/O Permanent Publications,
The Sustainability Centre, East Meon, Hampshire GU32 1HR
Email: info@permaculture.co.uk
Web. www.permaculture.co.uk
The author is available for consultancy on ecological building, and supplies chestnut
building products: roundwood building poles, riven chestnut laths and shingles

Brighton Tools and Fixings Ltd
Eardley House, 148 Carden Hill, Brighton, East Sussex BN1 8DD
Tel: 01273 562 020
Stainless steel fixings

Constructive Individuals
Trinity Pier, 64 Orchard Place, London E14 0JW
Tel: 0207 5159 299
Email: info@constructiveindividuals.com
Web: www.constructiveindividuals.com
Architects and Ecological Designers

Ecomerchant Ltd
Head Hill Road, Goodnestone, Faversham, Kent ME13 9BU
Tel: 01795 530 130
Web: www.ecomerchant.co.uk
Environmental builders merchants – Panelvent

Jeffrey Smith Associates
91 Ashfield Street, Whitechapel, London E1 2HA
Tel: 0207 2476 765
Fax: 0207 2472 110
Consulting Structural Engineers

Klober Limited
Pear Tree Industrial Estate, Upper Langford, Somerset BS40 5DJ
Tel: 01934 853 224/5
Web: www.klober.co.uk
Suppliers of Permaforte breathable membrane

Appendix V

Mike Wye and Associates
Buckland Filleigh Sawmills, Buckland Filleigh, Beaworthy, Devon EX21 5RN
Tel: 01409 281 644
Web: www.mikewye.co.uk
Lime, cob, ecological paints and building products

Onduline Building Products
Eardley House, 182-184 Campden Hill Road, Kensington, London W8 7AS
Tel: 020 7727 0533
Email: ondulineuk@aol.com
Suppliers of onduline roofing sheets

Paul Mills
Prestwick Farm, Nr. Chiddingfold, Surrey GU8 4XP
Tel: 01428 654 695
Supplier of building quality straw bales

Selkirk Manufacturing Ltd
Pottington Business Park, Barnstaple, Devon EX31 1LZ
Tel: 01271 326 633
Web: www.selkirk.co.uk
Chimney flues

Southern Solar Ltd
Unit 6, Allington Farm, Allington Lane, Offham, East Sussex BN7 3QL
Tel: 0845 456 9474
Web: www.southernsolar.co.uk
Suppliers, designers and installers of solar water and solar electric systems

Stephen F Morley
Photographer
Harthanger House, Lodsworth, West Sussex GU28 9BZ
Email: steve@stephenstills.demon.co.uk
Steve has an archive collection of photographs of the construction of the woodland house and is the author's photographic agent

Velux Group
Woodside Way, Glenrothes East, Fife KY7 4ND
Tel: 01592 772 211
Web: www.velux.co.uk
Roof windows

WT Anchor Systems
21 Phoenix Place Industrial Estate, Lewes, East Sussex BN7 2QJ
Tel: 01273 479 764
Web: www.duckbill-ground-anchors.co.uk
Suppliers of earth anchors

Drawings

Appendix VI

Side Elevation (South)
Front Elevation (West)
Side Elevation (North)
Rear Elevation (East)
Plan
Cross Section AA
Cross Section BB
Cross Section CC
Foundation Plan
Bale Plan

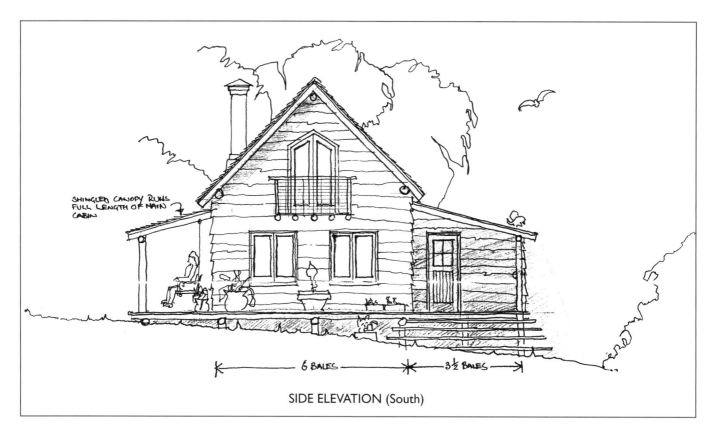

SHINGLED CANOPY RUNS
FULL LENGTH OF MAIN
CABIN

|← —— 6 BALES —— →|← 3½ BALES →|

SIDE ELEVATION (South)

FRONT ELEVATION (West)

SIDE ELEVATION (North)

REAR ELEVATION (East)

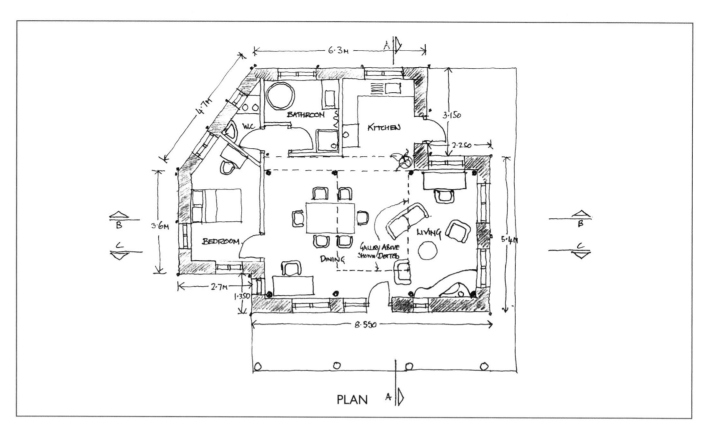

PLAN

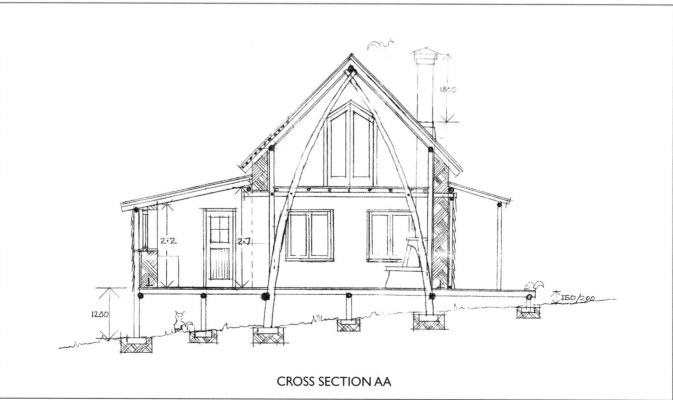

CROSS SECTION AA

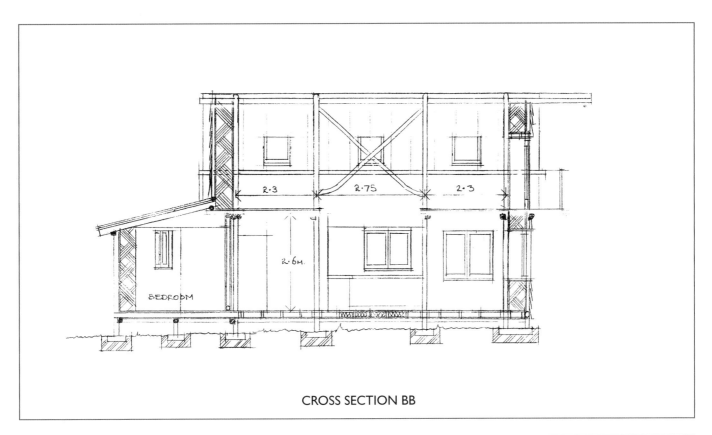

CROSS SECTION BB

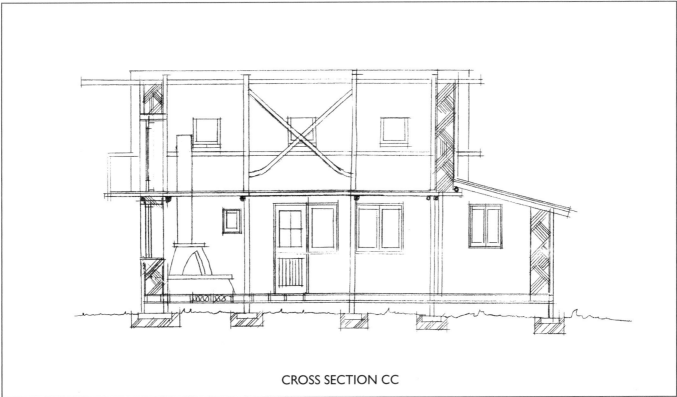

CROSS SECTION CC

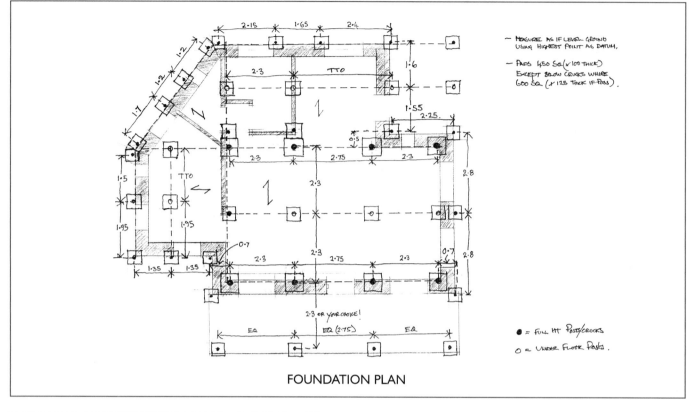

- MEASURE AS IF LEVEL GROUND USING HIGHEST POINT AS DATUM.
- PADS 450 SQ (x 100 THICK) EXCEPT BELOW CRUCKS WHERE 600 SQ (x 125 THICK IF POSS)

● = FULL HT POSTS/CRUCKS

O = UNDER FLOOR POSTS.

FOUNDATION PLAN

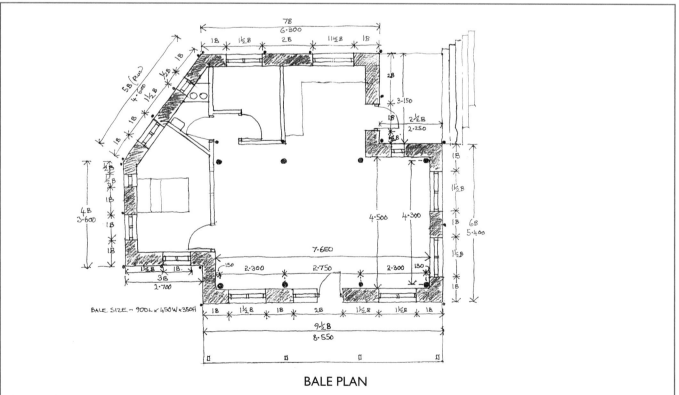

BALE SIZE - 900L x 450W x 350H

BALE PLAN

Engineer's Calculations

Reprinted from part of the engineer's report and given one full set of calculations for a beam. All beams were calculated using this formula.

The calculations for this woodland cabin is to be constructed as a cruck frame with lean-to elements around much of the perimeter of post and beam construction. The external walls are to have straw bale infill with a timber board rain screen. All supporting posts to sit on stone foundation pads.

The main structural timbers are to be sweet chestnut 'in the round'. To simplify the calculations, square sections have been used for analysis. These have been taken as the square section that will fit inside the average diameter of the round section. For example, 70x70 within a 100 diameter. Grade TH2 Oak has been shown to be satisfactory. Table 1 in BRE Digest 445 shows that Sweet Chestnut grade TH1 is very similar in properties to Oak of Grade TH2. We have therefore assumed that the timber 'in the round' will have the additional strength to make up the difference.

Conversations with TRADA and Department of Wood Science at the University of Surrey anticipated that timber in the round would be up to 50% stronger.

This is an unusual property in its construction and intended use. Some standard acceptable limits are not as relevant here as is usually the case. This is particularly true with deflection limits. There will be no hard plaster surfaces in the house. The owner/occupier will also be the builder. For these reasons and the fact that timber 'in the round' will be stronger than the calculations allow for, it is considered reasonable to accept greater design deflections than current standards include for.

Loadings:

Roof			
	Dead Load	**Live Load**	**Entire Load**
Shingles	0.20		
Battens	0.05		
Rafters	0.20		
Insulation	0.10		
9mm Panelvent	0.15		
Live		0.75	
Total	0.70	0.75	1.45kN/m²

Ground Floor			
	Dead Load	Live Load	Entire Load
Oak Boards	0.18		
Joists	0.25		
Insulation	0.05		
9mm Panelvent	0.15		
Live		1.50	
Total	0.63	1.50	2.13kN/m^2

Roundwood			
	Proposed Roundwood Diameter	Average	Equivalent Square Section
1 Cruck	260-150	200	141
2 Ridge	250-150	200	141
3 Eaves	210-125	168	119
4 Struts	130-170	150	106
5 Cruck Tie	150	150	106
6 Eaves	165-125	145	103
7 Post	165-125	145	103

Photo Credits

Photographers listed by page number

Appendix VIII

THE WOODLAND WAY
A Permaculture Approach
to Sustainable Woodland Management

This is for everyone who loves trees and woodlands...

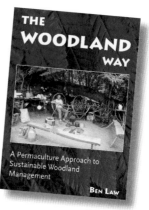

Written from the heart by an innovative woodsman who is deeply committed to sustainability, this radical book presents an immensely practical alternative to conventional woodland management. Through his personal experience, Ben Law clearly demonstrates how you can create biodiverse, healthy environments, yield a great variety of value added products, provide secure livelihoods for woodland workers and farmers, and benefit the local community. He argues the case for a new approach to planning, encouraging the creation of permaculture woodlands for the benefit of people, the local environment and the global climate.

ISBN 1 85623 009 0   235 x 165mm   256pp
116 black & white photos, 13 colour plates

Price: £16.95

"*Ben's brilliant book points the way forward for woodland management in the British Isles and beyond. It covers every aspect of what is in reality 'woodland stewardship', from both a practical and philosophical standpoint. This book is set to be a classic and will surely mark a turning point in our relationship with woods and the natural environment.*"

Jean-Paul Jeanrenaud
Formerly Head of the Forests for Life Programme,
WWF International.
Currently Head of the Business and Industry Programme, WWF International.
From the Foreword to *The Woodland Way*.

Permanent Publications
The Sustainability Centre, East Meon, Hampshire GU32 1HR, England
Tel: 0845 458 4150 or 01730 823 311 Fax: 01730 823 322
Email: orders@permaculture.co.uk Web: www.permaculture.co.uk

permaculture *magazine*

SOLUTIONS FOR SUSTAINABLE LIVING

Permaculture Magazine helps you live a more natural, healthy and environmentally friendly life.

Permaculture Magazine offers tried and tested ways of creating flexible, low cost approaches to sustainable living. It can help you to:

- **Make informed ethical choices**
- **Grow and source organic food**
- **Put more into your local community**
- **Build energy efficiency into your home**
- **Find courses, contacts and opportunities**
- **Live in harmony with people and the planet**

Permaculture Magazine is published quarterly for enquiring minds and original thinkers everywhere. Each issue gives you practical, thought provoking articles written by leading experts as well as fantastic eco-friendly tips from readers!

permaculture, ecovillages, organic gardening, sustainable agriculture, agroforestry, appropriate technology, eco-building, downshifting, community development, human-scale economy... and much more!

Permaculture Magazine gives you access to a unique network of people and introduces you to pioneering projects in Britain and around the world. Subscribe today and start enriching your life without overburdening the planet!

Every issue of Permaculture Magazine brings you the best ideas, advice and inspiration from people who are working towards a more sustainable world.

Permanent Publications
The Sustainability Centre, East Meon, Hampshire GU32 1HR, UK
Tel: 0845 458 4150 (local rate UK only) or +44 (0)1730 823 311
Fax: +44 (0)1730 823 322 Email: orders@permaculture.co.uk